We are writing these things so that
our joy may be complete…

1 John 1:4

Soul Rest

Lisa Donohue is a Christian Life, Hope, Stress and Grief Coach,
Advanced Board Certified by the American Association of Christian Counselors.
She is also a Grace-Focused Life Coach, certified by OMPC and Dr. Kenneth R. Jones.

Dedication & Acknowledgments

Whom else could I praise but the one who created me, inspired me, and continues to pursue me—my Abba Father.

To my husband, Steve, and our children, Ben, Hope, and Anna: Not many could endure a live-in church lady, but you have, and I am incredibly grateful for the time you've sacrificed, the grace you've offered, and the patience you've shown. I love you.

To Dr. Vaklavas: Thank you for asking about the writing.

Contents

A Personal Introduction

Journaling has never been a forte of mine. It's only been in the last five years, after hearing of its benefits for years prior, that I've embraced its ability to transform what I see into the truth of what He's speaking. In other words, as I write, He speaks, and therefore I hear by the words that transform ink into life. In this way, journaling penetrates my mind, yes; but also my reason, spirit, and heart.

Is it supernatural? It must be. Only the Word can be heard through His word. It's a direct link to the soul you've been given. There is nothing quite so powerful. But, as I read His truth, and write His truth, the depth of transformation can be instantaneous one day and frustratingly distant the next. Why?

For me, I can honestly tell you that I will put other tasks to the front of my day. My mind may be present, but my spirit light years away anticipating the "what's next." Journaling takes time, a commodity I put earthly value to. It begs that I would linger in stillness, but my genetic make-up wonders, "How would that be productive?" Oh, for a heart that would honestly surrender to stillness and His presence more frequently.

But is it not all His, and can He not redeem anything, even time? Of course He can. God created time. Humans created clocks to maximize the time provided.

The minutes of my day tick away, and instead of pausing to commune with the Maker of time, I set my sights to mastering it. That's surely true of me. How about you?

It may be that journaling doesn't *feel* successful or worthy of your time. It may be that it is simply put it off until tomorrow, or just hoped for the best, regardless.

It may be that you've simply never learned how to dance with our Father through writing or journaling. I believe that may be the case for most. We've all picked up a blank notebook and stared at the pages, wondering where in the world to begin. Seriously, where does one begin?

With Scripture filling my heart to overflowing, journaling became breath for me in the midst of cancer. And so it began out of desperation. This would undoubtedly be the most intimate period of communicating with my Father that I had ever experienced.

Tuesdays were chemo days, and there were 18 of them. Late each Tuesday night, I would settle in for a communion infusion with God. While the rest of the world slept, we wrote.

It was rich, powerful, and filled me with hope and courage. It began with questions and conversation, and grew from there. For those hours alone, He was in the quiet, in the music, in the extension of my pen. The flow of this journal is not like any others I have found. It's a simple tool to guide your thoughts and prayers, to give your writing a springboard.

If this is your first time to experience such dedicated time with God, or the first time you have put words to the thoughts of your heart, enjoy the freedom of a new and unknown adventure. This journal is an incredibly personal expression. Your journal should not look or read like anyone else's simply because you were not created like anyone else. The intimacy God wants to create with you is for you only. I pray you find peace in trusting Him fully with who you are and what you're experiencing.

More importantly, I hope you experience more of who He is and His purpose for where you are in this season of life.

If you are a seasoned journal writer, enjoy the beauty and refreshed transformation of your heart. Not that the journal has any transforming power, but time in His Word does. I pray this will bring new life, new perspective, and fresh hope to your soul.

My desire is that you'll experience the transforming power of a living God within your soul. You will quickly realize that you are not alone. Oh, how intimately the Father knows you, and even more, how much He loves you. He abides within the pages you read and the very letters you write.

He seeks to heal and restore your heart; you need to simply be still. Are you willing?

In returning and rest

you shall be saved;

in quietness and trust

shall be your strength.

But you were unwilling…

Isaiah 30:15

Elements of Your Prayer Journal

Elements of Your Prayer Journal

Time

Time alone is a sacrifice that even Jesus found necessary, yet we minimize its redeeming value. *Allow a minimum of 2-3 hours if you want to complete this journal in one sitting. However, if you have the freedom, linger through this over the course of an entire day. Don't have time today? Make a date for yourself!

If this journal is used throughout the course of several days, it is of upmost importance that every time you begin, you start with Preparing Your Heart. You may want to allow even more time to praise and worship on your own once completed with the directed portions. Trust Him with your heart, your time.

(Don't freak out about the time commitment. This is the part where I remind you that God created time.)

Space

You are precious to God, uniquely made in His image. He wants all of you, not just a piece of you.

Therefore, lock yourself in a room, find a bench at the park, sit on the beach, go to your back porch, stay in bed, but give yourself the freedom to be fully you, fully alone with Him.

Anticipate interruptions wherever your space may be, but fight the inclination to respond.

Position

Your position before the Lord will be reflective of your heart. Therefore, take this time in solitude to stand and raise your arms, or to kneel before Him with palms open in surrender. Be at rest, you are being held.

The worship set suggested at the end will be worthy of great expressions of joy. Sit, lie down, kneel, bow, dance…scripture displays all positions; it is all good, very good.

Music & Worship

Since ancient days, music and worship have been the elements that precede, intercede, and conclude all spiritual battles. Why would we not use this wonderfully powerful gift to help us engage and focus, all while keeping our hearts lifted and surrendered?

Scientists have learned that the positive and negative streams to your mind work differently. While the negative thoughts have a direct path, the positive thoughts must go through a filter. In other words, you're not the only one whose thoughts go negative first and in our flesh, quite normal.

Let's repeat this game-changer. Your positive thoughts must go through a filter; the negative thoughts have a green light. This heightens the significance of the scripture, "take **every** thought captive to Christ." Are my thoughts representative of what the living God proclaims? Often, they are more a reflection of my earthly sin nature. Fear, guilt, shame, control, and pride are all breeding grounds for negativity.

But God has given us the battle plan. Does He not send the worshippers into battle first? (*2 Chronicles 20:20-23*)

We, too, can implore the tools of the Ancient of Days to help us break through the battlefields in our mind first, before God quickens our heart. In some spiritual way, instrumental music keeps our thoughts balanced, thereby blocking our ability to stray.

Because this is your time in solitude, take time to settle into your journal with worship. Let me repeat that… take t-i-m-e to worship first. What leads your heart to worship may not be what leads my heart to worship, and that's fine! There are no rules. It's simply a tool to further open your mind and heart to His glorious unfolding.

Playlists for the Prayer Journal

There are playlists (soundtracks) to accompany each of the three sections of the journal: Preparing Your Heart, Exploring Your Heart, and Worship from Your Heart. Each is purposeful. Each is intentional.

Simply put, the playlists will be displayed as Preparing Your Heart, Exploring Your Heart, and Worship from Your Heart. **In advance**, you may choose to download the playlists or simply be prepared to listen via Spotify, YouTube, iTunes, Pandora, etc.

Particularly during the Exploring Your Heart segment, you may want to set up Pandora or Spotify with, for example, David Tolk, and let it run continuously, or loop, from there. Extended time of peace with instrumental background will be your friend. And not only your friend, but partner as it allows you to stay fully present with the guided questions and conversations.

You have control of the pace and have the option to replay the musical piece to remain in a particular section of the journal, or to continue into the next musical piece and/or section.

Direction

Each segment has its own playlist and its own set of questions. Let the music lead you through a series of questions, or conversations, with God. He has directed the questions just as much as He has directed you here. But don't assume that the music will always pace your writing. Simply, if you want to linger in one section longer than the playlist allows, do it.

There will be direction as you go. Stop and take a deep breath. Surrender control. It's okay.

Scripture

Some of the Scripture will be presented as first person so that you can read it as written to **you**. It will be presented from differing versions of the Bible. Receive it; don't let the process interfere with the results.

Notebook

You might choose to write in a separate notebook, allowing for multiple days of solitude from each journal. Each time you begin, go through the "Let's get started" checklist. You may want to date each day as memory stones of his faithfulness.

Elements of Your Prayer Journal, con't.

Now, access the music below via Spotify, Pandora, iTunes, etc. You will be instructed when to start the music and once you do, loop the tracks within each section as often as you'd like!

Preparing Your Heart

Restless, Audrey Assad
Rest Upon Us, Caedmon's Call

Exploring Your Heart

In Reverence, David Tolk
Grace, David Tolk
For Lisa, David Tolk

Worship from Your Heart

I Call You Jesus, Israel Houghton (& New Breed)
Good Good Father, Chris Tomlin
Jesus Messiah, Chris Tomlin
Glorious Day, Casting Crowns,
Power of Your Love, Hillsong Worship
Hello, My Name Is, Matthew West

Once you have your playlist easily accessible, turn the page.

Now, get a glass of water/coffee/tea. Use the restroom if you think it will cause you to stop processing in the next hour or two… not kidding.

Make sure you have at least one pen (get a backup if possible!).

Look at your phone one more time; turn on 'do not disturb,' or turn it off and just walk away. You can do it!

Find a place of absolute solitude.

Once you find your space, you have easy access to the playlist, and you are settled, continue.

Take a minute to write any last minute "things to remember" before we clear the slate. You have the freedom to come back to this list when you're finished. It could be task reminders, grocery lists, calls you need to make, or anything that might distract.

Once you're finished with this list, turn the page.

Things I want to remember before I start:

Preparing Your Heart

PREPARING YOUR HEART

Now, begin playing the "Preparing Your Heart" playlist

Start letting go of daily thoughts, lists, appointments, and your own expectations.

Let your heartbeat slow.

Calm your breathing.

Find stillness.

Hear His invitation and trust that the doors of your heart will be opened.

Take a deep breath in, and exhale.

Take a deep breath in, and exhale.

Take a deep breath in, and invite The Lord into your space.

Remain quiet for the duration of these 2 songs, taking note of the words that He may be speaking to you. Feel free to doodle, write, or draw on this page or the following page.

Oh Lord, all my longing is before you; my sighing is before you.   Psalm 38:9

Pause. Continue only after you have fully exhaled, or simply when you are ready. Don't rush your heart.

Exploring Your Heart

EXPLORING YOUR HEART

Now, begin playing the "Exploring Your Heart" playlist
(Loop tracks as little or as often as you wish.)

This is your time to be intimately alone with the One who calls **you** His.

This One, He is your Father;
your burden bearer;
your very spirit, your very joy;
your most intimate and safe Friend.

He is the One,
the One who feeds your soul;
the One who lifts your arms;
the One who redeems your life, heals your heart,
fills your empty places and quickens your heart.

This One is Jesus.

Lord God and Father, I would be lying if I didn't confess the weariness of my heart.

I know that this side of heaven promises that I will experience both the cup of joy and the cup of suffering… especially for the one who is called into fellowship with You.

But it is so hard to trust.

How can these very trials be designed to draw me into greater love and communion with You, Father?

You know me. You see me. You hear me. You abide within me. Walk me into the freedom You offer me through the sufferings of Christ. You are my redeemer, the only true hope in the world.

I have been crucified with Christ. It is no longer I who live, but Christ who lives in me. And the life I now live in the flesh I live by faith in the Son of God, who loved me and gave himself for me. Galatians 2:20

The heaviness of my heart, the burden that I carry, is not foreign to You, Father. You know my frustration, despair, and pain. In fact, it was for the joy set before your Son (who endured the cross, despising the shame, and is now seated next to You, at Your right hand) that I can be free of these burdens. Father, I am the joy He set to redeem as He endured the cross. Help me to see.

Help me to believe.

What great love, that He would love me to the point of His earthly death, buying back for me my life in His. And not only to redeem me for eternity, but to offer me freedom to be released from the weightiness of the trials of life on this side…

freedom from wanting to control,

freedom from guilt and shame,

freedom from the pain of lost dreams and prolonged hopes,

freedom from being incapable and unable to fix the hurt,

and freedom from fear of the "what if."

It was for freedom that Christ set us free. Galatians 5:1

Lord, I would love freedom from….

Help me to experience Your nearness through Christ, and the washing of my heart so that I am restored and at rest.

Oh Lord, restore the joy of Your salvation to my tired and weary heart. If my heart were restored, it would feel or look like:

I came that they may have life and have it abundantly. John 10:10

Come, friend, this is your tent of meeting. Let's do more writing.

Know that the Lord, he is God! It is He who made us, and we are his; we are his people and the sheep of his pasture. Enter his gates with thanksgiving and his courts with praise! Give thanks to him; bless his name! Psalm 100: 3-4

You are God, the Everlasting One. You created me; you created me for you and for your glory. How wonderful are *your* works.

You are the Great I AM.

You are the Alpha and Omega.

You are my..........

*What marvelous love the Father has given to me, that I should be called a **true** child of God, and so I am. 1 John 3:1*

(Repeat verse aloud, if even in a whisper. Put a voice to it, and repeat it until your mind and *heart* hear it.)

Father, gently walk through the corridors of my heart.

*The Lord is **my** shepherd; I shall not want. He makes me lie down in green pastures. He leads me beside still waters. He restores my soul. He leads me in paths of righteousness for his name's sake. Psalm 23:1-3*

As I read the verse above, Lord, it reveals Your protection, Your goodness. It promises that in *my* life,

1. You... *(lead me beside still waters, for example)*

2. You...

3. You...

4. You...

As I consider these things, I can see how you have accomplished these four promises in my life by:

(For example: You make me to lie down in green pastures by reminding me that I am safe in your arms if nowhere else. In you there is no fear, no darkness, and rest is mine.)

1.

2.

3.

4.

You are trustworthy. Even now, I continue to surrender my heart to You, the only One who offers me life. I am safe, protected, and loved in Your space.

If I were to be completely honest, Lord, there are so many things on my mind…

[Alternate starting phrases: I just don't understand how… I don't understand why… What if…. I am completely overwhelmed with/by...]

But in this moment, or today, the single biggest issue on my heart is:

I want to believe that you're in control, and that you are good. But in my heart, what I honestly believe is:

And what I'm experiencing is:

If only that was the bottom of the well, but it's not. If I am really honest, what I feel even more deeply about this situation is:

Because of what I'm believing (what I just wrote), what I'm feeling is:

Do you see the despair, and yet thankfulness, of my heart, Lord?

In my heart of hearts, Lord, I want to fix everything instead of turning it over to you completely.

But the load is heavy, and I am tired.

Father, it's awful to feel so stuck, so focused on everything except your truth, your promises, and your steadfast love.

Right now, in this moment, I confess that I am focused on things that are not life-giving. They may even be self-centered, though I never intended for them to be.

These "things" or feelings are not ever going to offer me the hope I have in you. I need you.

I.

Need.

You.

I need the truth of your promises and the hope of your steadfast love to completely destroy every negative thought and untruth that has taken control of my mind.

I sit before you, in the silence of my heart. Only you know me in this deep place. *Pause, breathe deep, and exhale just as deep.*

Give yourself space/time to remember scripture, write truth, and to reflect on what you've already written.

Of these confessions and burdens, Lord, I surrender.

In my unbelief, I assumed control of:

And in fear, or maybe even because of my pride, I have strived to:

Forgive me, Father; my transgressions lie before you. I have assumed the role of God in so many situations in my life, and it's too much.

You are the only wise King. Only You offer true wisdom. Let my mind stay steadfast on Your truth.

  With You as *my* King, I believe…

You are the Prince of Peace. In Your presence, all my fears are washed away.

  With You as *my* Prince of Peace, I trust You to…

You are *my* Wonderful Counselor. In You are wisdom and honor.

  With You as my wonderful Counselor, I feel….

You are *my* redeemer, and the only One who redeems and restores.

  You have redeemed/restored…

You are *my* Father. Only You have conquered death, and only You can conquer the power of sin in my life.

Blessed is the one whose transgression is forgiven, whose sin is covered. Blessed is the man against whom the Lord counts no iniquity, and in whose spirit there is no deceit. For when I kept silent, my bones wasted away through my groaning all day long. Psalm 32:1-3

Since therefore the children share in the flesh and blood, he himself likewise partook of the same things, that through death he might destroy the one who has the power of death, that is, the devil. Hebrews 2:14

And Jesus cried out and said, "Whoever believes in me, believes not in me but in him who sent me. And whoever sees me sees him who sent me. I have come into the world as light, so that whoever believes in me may not remain in darkness." John 12:44-46

For the law of the Spirit of life has set you free in Christ Jesus from the law of sin and death. Romans 8:2

*For you are my lamp, O Lord, and my God lightens my darkness.
2 Samuel 22:29*

Father, wash me anew with Your holy presence. Restore my faith in You, not in things of this earth.

Create in me a clean heart, oh Lord.

Formerly, when you did not know God, you were enslaved to those that by nature are not gods. Galatians 4:8 (fear, pride, control, shame)

But God...

In him we have redemption through his blood, the forgiveness of our trespasses, according to the riches of his grace. Ephesians 1:7

The Lord is not slow to fulfill his promises as some count slowness,
  but is patient toward you,
    not wishing that any should perish,
      but that all should reach repentance.
        2 Peter 3:9

I acknowledged my sin to you, and I did not cover my iniquity; I said, "I will confess my transgressions to the Lord," and you forgave the iniquity of my sin. Psalm 32:5

Be glad in the Lord, and rejoice, O righteous, and shout for joy, all you upright in heart! Psalm 32:11

I have confessed the sin in my heart and entrusted it to You, Father. The washing of Christ's blood over my sin redeems my soul from the pit and offers me fresh breath, new mercies, new life.

I am not my sin and I am not my circumstance.

I am Yours.

In Christ, I am your blameless, beloved, redeemed, adopted, and chosen child.

I, _____, have been set free!

I, _____, truly am a child of God!

Yes, I am His and He is mine. I have been reconciled; I have a family that extends to the ends of the earth and to eternity. Because of who You are, I can trust You. Praise You, Lord!

Now I know the joy of grace, it is truly amazing. *For by grace you have been saved through faith. And this is not your own doing; it is the gift of God. Ephesians 2:8*

See what kind of love the Father has given to us, that we should be called the children of God; and so we are. 1 John 3:1

In your great mercy Father, you…

In your great power Father, you can…

Father, I can trust you because…

Father, I lift all this up to you with a hearty Amen!

Selah

Worship from Your Heart

WORSHIP FROM YOUR HEART

Now, begin playing the "Worship from Your Heart" playlist
(loop tracks as little or as often as you wish)

The LORD your God is in your midst, a mighty one who will save; he will rejoice over you with gladness; he will quiet you by his love; he will exult over you with loud singing. Zephaniah 3:17

Lord, this is what Your freedom and love feel like to me:

The scripture, or promise, which revived my heart and the one I don't want to forget, is:

Selah

Scripture References

SCRIPTURE REFERENCES

We are writing these things so that our joy may be complete. 1 John 1:4

In returning and rest you shall be saved; in quietness and trust shall be your strength. But you were unwilling… Isaiah 30:15

O Lord, all my longing is before you; my sighing is before you. Psalm 38:9

I have been crucified with Christ. It is no longer I who live, but Christ who lives in me. And the life I now live in the flesh I live by faith in the Son of God, who loved me and gave himself for me. Galatians 2:20

It was for freedom that Christ set me free. Galatians 5:1

I came that they might have life and have it abundantly. John 10:10

Know that the Lord, he is God! It is he who made us, and we are his; we are his people and the sheep of his pasture. Enter his gates with thanksgiving and his courts with praise! Give thanks to him; bless his name! Psalm 100: 3-4

What marvelous love the Father has given to me, that I should be called a true child of God, and I am. 1 John 3:1

The Lord is my shepherd; I shall not want. He makes me lie down in green pastures. He leads me beside still waters. He restores my soul. He leads me in paths of righteousness for his name's sake. Psalm 23:1-3

Blessed is the one whose transgression is forgiven, whose sin is covered. Blessed is the man against whom the Lord counts no iniquity, and in whose spirit there is no deceit. For when I kept silent, my bones wasted away through my groaning all day long. Psalm 32:1-3

Since therefore the children share in the flesh and blood, he himself likewise partook of the same things, that through death he might destroy the one who has the power of death, that is, the devil. Hebrews 2:14

And Jesus cried out and said, "Whoever believes in me, believes not in me but in him who sent me. And whoever sees me sees him who sent me. I have come into the world as light, so that whoever believes in me may not remain in darkness." John 12:44-46

For the law of the Spirit of life has set you free in Christ Jesus from the law of sin and death. Romans 8:2

For you are my lamp, O Lord, and my God lightens my darkness. 2 Samuel 22:29

I acknowledged my sin to you, and I did not cover my iniquity; I said, "I will confess my transgressions to the Lord," and you forgave the iniquity of my sin. Psalm 32:5

Be glad in the Lord, and rejoice, O righteous, and shout for joy, all you upright in heart! Psalm 32:11

Formerly, when you did not know God, you were enslaved to those that by nature are not gods. Galatians 4:8

In him we have redemption through his blood, the forgiveness of our trespasses, according to the riches of his grace. Ephesians 1:7

The Lord is not slow to fulfill his promises as some count slowness, but is patient toward you, not wishing that any should perish, but that all should reach repentance. 2 Peter 3:9

This is the message that we have heard from him and proclaim to you, that God is light, and in him is no darkness at all. 1 John 1:5

For by grace you have been saved through faith. And this is not your own doing; it is the gift of God. Ephesians 2:8

See what kind of love the Father has given to us, that we should be called the children of God; and so we are. 1 John 3:1

The LORD your God is in your midst, a mighty one who will save; he will rejoice over you with gladness; he will quiet you by his love; he will exult over you with loud singing. Zephaniah 3:17

About the Author

Lisa and her husband, Steve, currently live in Birmingham, Alabama. They have three beautiful children and a puppy.

Lisa is the founder of Stonewashed Authentic Life Coaching, where she offers coaching for life, hope, cancer, stress management, and grief as an Advanced Board Certified Christian Life Coach. You can contact her by emailing lisa@stonewashedllc.com, and you can read more about her services by going to www.stonewashedllc.com.

72983762R00027